101 ROMANTIC IDEAS

ANURADHA SRIVASTAVA

Contents

Prologue

101 ROMANTIC IDEAS
by Michael Webb

IDEA # 1

If your partner is going away for a few days, tell her that you are worried about her so you have organized a bodyguard to look after her. Then give her a small teddy bear.

IDEA # 2

Buy a packet of glow in the dark stars and stick the stars on the roof above your bed to spell out a message such as "I Love You" When the lights go down, your message will be revealed!

IDEA # 3

On a special occasion, buy your partner eleven real red roses and one artificial red rose. Place the artificial rose in the center of the bouquet.

Attach a card that says:
"I will love you until the last rose fades."

IDEA # 4

Buy the domain name of your partner's name if it is available for example. Create a web page containing a romantic poem and a picture of a rose. When your partner is surfing the web, casually ask whether she has ever checked to see whether her domain name is taken. Let her type it in to discover her page.

IDEA # 5

Buy a stylish hand mirror and give it to your partner as a gift. Include a card in the box saying

> "In this mirror you will see the image of the most beautiful woman in the world."

IDEA # 6

Take a book that your partner is reading and using a pencil, underline letters in a section of the book she has yet to read to spell out a love letter. For example in the following exert from a novel, the underlined letters come together to spell out the secret message "I love you"

> The palace was a labyrinth, their passage through it tortuous and interminable. Initially they passed from building to building under the sodden sky. Steve's feet ached; he might have laughed at himself, the tireless traveler, grown too soft from his months in the city to walk any proper distance. Abruptly the guards halted.

> The underlined letters will make your partner curious and with a bit of luck she will write them down. Spend time to encode a proper message such as "Dear Belinda, I love you honey"

IDEA # 7

Have flowers delivered to your partner's workplace. She will not only enjoy the flowers but will also receive comments and attention from her office mates which will add to her enjoyment.

IDEA # 8

While walking with your partner on a weekend getaway, pick up a smooth stone and say that you're going to keep it as a special memento of your trip.

Later, have a message such as
"I Love Rebecca"
engraved into the stone by a jeweler and give it to your partner.

IDEA # 9

Drive into the country, find a grassy hill and lie with your partner and look up at the clouds.

Play the kid's game of looking for shapes in the cloud formations.

IDEA # 10

Get a piece of paper and some crayons. Draw a bright childlike picture with a smiley sun and two stick figures holding hands. Add labels with your two names pointing to the stick figures. Write "I Love You" inside a heart.

Next get a large formal envelope. Place your drawing inside and type up a formal address label of your partner's work such as:

For the immediate and urgent attention of:
Rebecca Jones Level 20
Collins & Smith Solicitors New York

Mail it to your partner so she receives it in the middle of a busy day.

IDEA # 11

Memorize one of Shakespeare's love sonnets and recite it to your partner when you are in a romantic setting like a botanical garden. Don't just suddenly start reciting poetry as this will just sound corny.

While you are cuddling your partner, ask in a joking manner, "So is now a good time to recite a love poem to you?" She will probably say yes, expecting you to come up with something of the "Roses are Red..." variety.

Instead, look into her eyes, smile and recite the sonnet while you gently stroke her face. Try the sonnet below. If this is too long, just memorize the first four lines and the last two.

Shakespeare Love Sonnet 18

Shall I compare thee to a summer's day? Thou art more lovely and more temperate.

Rough winds do shake the darling buds of May, And summer's lease hath all too short a date.

Sometime too hot the eye of heaven shines, And often is his gold complexion dimmed, And every fair from fair sometime declines,

By chance or nature's changing course untrimmed. But thy eternal summer shall not fade,

Nor lose possession of that fair thou owest,

Nor shall Death brag thou wander'st in his shade

When in eternal lines to time thou grow'st.

So long as men can breathe, or eyes can see, So long lives this, and this gives life to thee.

IDEA # 12

If your partner has to work late, take a lunch box and fill it with some of her favorite things such as chocolates, herbal tea, cookies, a small teddy bear.

Next, get a piece of paper and write

"Michelle's Late Night Survival Pack"

Draw a big red cross below this and stick the paper to the top of the box. Tell your partner to open the box when things get really tough.

IDEA # 13

If you are walking by a park, visit the swings and give your partner a ride. This will often bring back happy memories from her childhood.

IDEA # 14

Leave a long stem rose where your partner will find it with a note on it saying: "Thank you for coming into my life."

IDEA # 15

If your partner is starting a new job, buy a copy of "The Sound Of Music" sound track. Tape the song, "I Have Confidence" onto a tape and add your own message at the end of the song saying,

"Good Luck honey, I have confidence in you." Give the tape to your partner to play on the way to work in the car.

IDEA # 16

Buy a small decorated cardboard box, a sheet of colored tissue paper, some massage oil and a blank card.

Line the box with the tissue paper. Place the massage oil in the box and write the following message on the card:

I know a great Masseur. For an appointment ring:
(Your Phone Number)

IDEA # 17

When your spouse has had a really long hard day, run a hot bath for her. Pour some fragrant bath oil into the tub and gently bathe her from head to toe. Carry her into the bedroom. Gently towel her dry and tuck her into a freshly made bed with a kiss on the forehead.

IDEA # 18

For this idea you will need a portable CD player. If you and your partner have a favorite song, get a copy of it on CD and take it with you when you go away for a romantic weekend.

When you are in a romantic spot, ask your partner if she would like to dance. Place one earpiece in her ear and one in your own and enjoy your private dance floor.

This technique is particularly effective if the romantic spot you have chosen is somewhere where people would not normally dance, for example, the top of the Empire State building at sunset or on top of a mountain during a camping trip.

IDEA # 19

If your partner has a pet that she adores, at Christmas, in addition to buying a gift for your partner, buy a small present for her pet.

IDEA # 20

Go for a walk on the beach. Trace out the shape of a large love heart in the sand. Sit inside the heart and cuddle your partner as you watch the sun go down.

IDEA # 21

Invite your partner to go for a walk. Get a back pack and pack the following items: A picnic blanket, a selection of fruit in small containers eg. strawberries, grapes, watermelon and kiwi fruit. Some cheese and crackers. Some sandwiches. A small tin of caviar. A half bottle of champagne and two plastic champagne glasses. If your partner asks what's in the backpack, just say a jacket and some lunch.

When you find a romantic spot, ask if she would like to stop for a bite to eat. Open your pack and remove the items one by one to set up your picnic. The last item you remove should be the glasses and champagne.

IDEA # 22

If you play a musical instrument, create a romantic environment in which to play for your partner. For example, let's say you play the saxophone. Contact your partner's roommate and arrange for her to make sure that your partner steps out onto the balcony of their apartment at exactly 9.30PM.

Drive to her apartment and set up before hand. Place a large sparkler in the music holder of your sax and light it as your partner steps on to the balcony. Play something slow and romantic.

IDEA # 23

Use this idea if your partner is going to work and you are staying at home for some reason (Perhaps you are sick or are working from home).

Say goodbye to her at the front door and then immediately send an email to her work address. The email should simply say,

"Miss you already".

The email will be in her in-box when she does her morning email check.

IDEA # 24

If your partner has long hair, take the time to brush it using long slow strokes. This is particularly effective after she has had a shower or when she is getting ready for bed.

IDEA # 25

On a special occasion like your partner's birthday, plan a treasure hunt for her. The fun begins when you suggest going for a walk on the beach.

When you get to the beach, carry a small bag with you. The bag contains a bottle that you prepared earlier. Inside the bottle is a treasure map. To make the treasure map look authentic, burn the edges with a match.

As you are walking, slip the bottle out of your bag and let it drop to the sand near the water's edge. You may have to pause and kiss your partner to do this unnoticed. Walk a little further up the beach then turn around and retrace your steps to 'discover' the bottle.

On the map have a dotted line leading from the beach to a nearby cafe. At the cafe, your partner won't know what to look for so suggest that you just sit down and have a cup of coffee.

When the waitress delivers the coffee, she suggests to your partner that she might find what she is looking for under the coaster. When your partner turns over the coaster she finds a key taped to the bottom. Obviously you will have to set this up before hand with the waitress. Most waitresses will be happy to help a romantic guy out with this type of thing.

At the next stop on the map, your partner finds or is given a spade. Then at the last stop on the map your partner finds a large 'X' made up of two crossed sticks. She digs and discovers a locked box. The key unlocks the box to reveal her present.

IDEA # 26

Invite your partner on a date by sending her a plain brown envelope containing a tape. On the tape, record the Mission Impossible sound track and then record yourself saying, "Your mission if you choose to accept it is to make your way to Café Venoli, 123 Park Lane at 18.30 Eastern Standard Time. There you will rendezvous with a stunningly attractive man wearing a red carnation. The future of the free world is now in your hands. This tape will self destruct in five seconds." Then record <u>ten</u> beeps from a stopwatch and record yourself saying, "Would you believe ten seconds..." Its corny but it usually gets a laugh!

IDEA # 27

Contact your partner's family and ask if there was anything she always wanted when she was a little girl.

For example if she always wanted a porcelain doll, buy one for her birthday. She will not only appreciate the gift but also the fact that you were thoughtful enough to find out what she always wanted.

IDEA # 28

Organize a professional photo shoot to obtain a portrait of the two of you as a couple. Frame the picture and put it somewhere prominent. Remember to make sure you give your partner plenty of notice so that she can get ready.

IDEA # 29

Write a note saying

"I thought of you today, and it made me smile." Leave the note somewhere where your partner is sure to find it.

IDEA # 30

For Valentines Day, buy your partner a charm bracelet with at least 14 charms.

Remove all the charms and let your partner 'find' one charm each day for the first fourteen days of February. On Valentines Day give her the bracelet and any remaining charms.

IDEA # 31

When you and your partner are in a shopping center or airport, stop at one of those booths that allow you to take an instant photo and print them out as stickers.

Choose a romantic background and kiss your partner while the photo is being taken.

IDEA # 32

If your partner has voice mail at work or on her mobile, leave a message saying

"Just wanted to let you know that I'm thinking of you." She will appreciate this anytime but especially when she is going through a rough period.

IDEA # 33

Organize a mystery trip for you and your partner. Some travel agents will organize mystery packages where the destination of the trip is kept secret until you are actually on the plane or arrive at the destination.

IDEA # 34

Buy some rose petals and place them behind the sun visor on the passenger side of your car. Take a post it note and write, "I Love You" on it and stick it to the back of the sun visor.

As you are driving to a romantic destination, look at your partner and tell her she has a mark on her cheek. She will pull down the sun visor to use the mirror and be showered in rose petals and see your note.

IDEA # 35

If your partner is going on a trip, pack a small present into the corner of her suitcase that she will find when she is away.

IDEA # 36

When you and your partner are having an anniversary, buy two champagne glasses and get them engraved with your names and the date, for example:

Mal and Kate

7 May 2002

Go to the restaurant where you have made your reservations and request that when you and your partner arrive that your champagne be served in your special glasses. This will be a great surprise for your partner and a wonderful keepsake for you both.

IDEA # 37

On a special occasion such as your partner's birthday, buy twenty-four red roses. Arrange to meet her at a specific spot in a shopping mall before going out for dinner. Get to the shopping mall early and position yourself around the corner from your meeting spot.

Ask a guy who is walking by whether he would mind helping you out. Give him a rose, point out your partner and ask him to walk up to her and say, "Happy Birthday Meagan" and give her the rose and then walk away. Repeat this with eleven other guys. Choose guys who are not too good looking and choose guys of different ages. A nice touch is to have the last rose delivered by a small child who could even by accompanied by his parents.

After the first twelve flowers have been delivered, approach your partner with the twelve remaining roses.

IDEA # 38

Always listen for things that your partner reminisces about and jot them down somewhere. For example, perhaps she talks about the ice cream that she had from a particular shop when she was a little girl.

When a special occasion comes along, check your list of things that your partner talks about and try to recreate one of them, for example, visit the shop and buy a tub of ice cream making sure that the name of the shop is on the container.

IDEA # 39

Create a love montage by collecting some photographs of you and your partner, some ticket stubs of places you have visited and any other small odds and ends that have special meaning to you both.

Take these items and get them professionally framed in a three dimensional montage. Alternatively, buy a frame and create a simple montage yourself.

IDEA # 40

Buy an ornately carved wooden box which is lined with green or red felt. Find an old fashioned key and place it in the box.

Next, get a small gold plaque and have it engraved with the words

The Key To My Heart

Fix the plaque to the inside of the top of the box so that it can be read when the box is opened.

IDEA # 41

Buy a tree with your partner and plant it in a special spot. Each year on your anniversary, have a glass of champagne next to your tree and talk about how your love and the tree have grown.

IDEA # 42

If you shower first in the morning. Steam up the bathroom and write a message such as "Pete Loves Kathy" on the mirror for your partner to read when she uses the bathroom. This also works on car windows when it's cold.

IDEA # 43

As a special gift, name a Star after your partner. A number of astronomical agencies allow individuals to name stars and you receive formal documentation identifying the star that you have named. See the following website for details:

Have you ever had a dull date? No more. This book features nearly 6 years worth of creative date nights. Tips on first dates and asking someone out for a date too.

IDEA # 44

Find a comic strip that relates to something that you and your partner have shared together, for example perhaps you both work in the same office and you find a Dilbert cartoon that relates to the politics at your workplace.

Enlarge the cartoon using a photocopier and use white-out to cover the cartoon text. Type up your own text that relates to you and your partner and paste it in the appropriate places and then photocopy the cartoon again so that it looks like your text was the actual text of the cartoon.

For an added touch, get your customized cartoon laminated before giving it to your partner.

IDEA # 45

When you and your partner are enjoying a restful time away, organize to wake up early one morning and go to a scenic spot to watch the sun rise.

This may seem difficult but it is something which is definitely worth doing at least once. Seeing a new day being born is something really special to share with your partner.

IDEA # 46

When you have access to a spa, create a romantic atmosphere by placing some candles around the tub and some rose petals floating on the surface of the water.

As your partner enjoys the water, serve champagne and chocolate covered strawberries before joining her.

IDEA # 47

Create some love coupons that your partner can exchange for romantic favors.

For example you could have a coupon that reads

This coupon entitles the bearer to:

One Foot Massage. Use by 07/08/2045

Use a date many years in the future if you want to suggest that you and your partner will always be together.

IDEA # 48

On a warm summers night, organize a backyard picnic. Spread a picnic blanket on the ground and get together some snacks, chocolates and champagne. Lie down on the blanket with your partner and gaze up at the stars together.

IDEA # 49

Next time it is raining really heavily, go for a walk with your partner. Forget the umbrellas and the raincoats. Run through the streets together, jump in puddles and get totally saturated.

Pick her up, twirl her around and kiss her while the rain falls. Taste the water off her face and hold her close.

When you get back home have a hot shower and then share a warm drink preferably in front of an open fire.

Organize a hot air ballooning trip as a special surprise. Most trips begin with a glass of champagne before you float over the countryside with your partner.

IDEA # 51

When your partner is sitting at a table or desk, come up behind him or her and give her a back, shoulder and head massage. Finish with a gentle kiss on the cheek.

IDEA # 52

Place an ad in the paper on a normal day saying something like:

Dear Amanda,
With you by my side, everyday feels like Valentines Day.
Thank you for being you. Love,
Graham

IDEA # 53

Buy a book that you and your partner are both interested in reading.

Read one chapter each night in bed with each of you taking turns to read out loud.

This can be a great alternative to television.

IDEA # 54

When your partner is having a shower or bath, take her towel and place it in the dryer to make it really warm and then wrap her up in it when she is done.

IDEA # 55

Photocopy your hand and fax a copy of it to your partner with a message saying, "Do ya wanna hold hands?"

IDEA # 56

Next time you order a pizza, ask to have it cut into a heart shape before it is delivered to your home.

IDEA # 57

Buy a box of chocolates and very carefully open one side of the plastic wrap so that you can gently slide the box out. Open the box and place a love note inside. Then slide the box back into its plastic wrap and reseal it.

IDEA # 58

Rent a tandem bike and go for a ride with your partner. At the end of your ride have a picnic in the park.

IDEA # 59

If you are away on a business trip, document a day in your life for your partner. For example:

'A Day In The Life Of Mark'

6AM: Just woke up and thought of you - Wish you were laying next to me. Well, I better get ready for work.

7AM: Am on the train. It's crowded; everyone looks like they are half dead. I miss ya heaps.

8.30AM: Have just organized my day, it's going to be a busy one.

9.30AM: Am in the middle of a really boring meeting. I am trying to concentrate on this months sales figures but I keep thinking of your beautiful eyes.

...

6.30PM: Thank goodness the day is over. I am counting the days until we're together again.

Send your letter to your partner. This is a wonderful way to tell your partner how often you think about her during the day and to share your life with her in a special way.

IDEA # 60

Speak to your partner's family and find out what her favorite book was when she was a little girl.

Buy a copy of the book and read it to her in bed.

IDEA # 61

Write an email story with your partner. Start the ball rolling with an email that says something like:

Chapter 1:

This is the story of Pete and Kate who met at a friend's engagement party one summer afternoon.

The email can then continue to develop the beginnings of a story which can be completely fictitious or a combination of fiction and reality.

Finish your email by saying, "And now for Chapter 2, its over to you..."

IDEA # 62

Buy a kite and on a windy day find a park and fly the kite with your partner.

If you can afford it, buy a large kite that you control with two hand lines. These kites are great fun.

IDEA # 63

When you and your partner are planning to go out for dinner, suggest that you have an 'Adventure Dinner'. Here's how it works

Set the timer on your stopwatch to count down twenty minutes. Next, ask your partner to choose a number between 5 and 10. Lets say she chooses 7.

Give your partner a coin and tell her that at every 7th intersection, she has to flip the coin. If it is heads you will turn left. If it is tails you will turn right.

When your watch timer goes off you have to both keep a look out for the nearest place to eat.

This is a fun way to get out and about and try new places to eat.

IDEA # 64

When you and your partner are going somewhere special, get your camera, buy a new roll of film and wait for her to come out of the house.

When she appears, act like a professional photographer and go wild taking pictures of her with the flash. While you are taking photos, bombard her with questions as though she was a famous actress and you are trying to get a scoop for the magazine you represent.

Not only is this fun but you will also get some great photos to look back on together.

IDEA # 65

When your partner is sick at home, take a day off to look after her.

Rent some videos, make her some soup, wrap her up in a blanket and just be with her.

IDEA # 66

When you are having dinner one night, ask your partner about the things she has always wanted to do.

Later on, write these things down so you don't forget them and over time try and help make them happen. For example she may say that one thing she has always wanted to do is swim with dolphins. Find out where she can do this and organize it for her as a special surprise.

IDEA # 67

Rent the video, "An Affair To Remember". Buy some popcorn, champagne and chocolate covered strawberries and have a special film night at home.

IDEA # 68

Go to the drive in but instead of sitting in the car, spread a picnic blanket on the ground. Light a candle and buy popcorn. Cuddle your partner and enjoy the film.

IDEA # 69

Create a personalized magazine cover for your partner. To do this, get hold of a good quality photo of her and a copy of a popular entertainment magazine.

Take these two items to a print shop or graphic design agency. Ask them to scan your partner's photo and develop a magazine cover with the lead story being, "The

30 most beautiful women of 2003".

When you get the cover, stick it on the front of a real magazine and ask your local shop owner whether you can place it in the magazine rack. Organize to meet your partner at the shop before going out. When she arrives, tell her that you are just looking for a magazine. Let her browse the rack and discover her magazine.

IDEA # 70

Fill the trunk of your car with helium balloons. Drive to a romantic spot in the country to go for a walk. The ideal spot is somewhere up high with a clear view of the surrounding countryside.

Get out of the car and act as though you are about to set off for your walk. Make sure your partner is closer to the car than you and then throw her the keys and ask if she can get your jacket from the trunk while you tie your shoelace.

When she opens the boot the balloons will be released. You can also place a sign saying, "I Love You" on the inside of the trunk so that it will be revealed when the trunk opens.

IDEA # 71

On a special occasion create a unique present for your partner by buying two white t-shirts and some fabric paint. Draw half a heart and the letters LO on one t-shirt and the half a heart and the letters VE on the other t-shirt.

When you walk down the street holding each other close, the heart will be made whole and your message of love revealed.

IDEA # 72

On a hot summers day, buy two large water pistols and take them to the beach with you.

Pull them out and throw one to your partner and then have a huge water fight.

IDEA # 73

Share your food with your partner. When you go out for a meal, hold a forkful up to her mouth and say, "You've got to try this."

Sharing your food and even feeding each other is a great way to become closer as a couple.

IDEA # 74

Compliment your partner in public. If you are talking in a group and it is appropriate to the conversation say something like, "Kate makes the most incredible roast." Squeeze her hand while you are talking about her.

IDEA # 75

Arrange a special day off from work. Start with breakfast, go for a walk in the park, go shopping, have afternoon tea in a cozy cafe and finish off with a romantic dinner.

IDEA # 76

Buy a gift voucher for a facial at a local beauty clinic and place it in a card accompanied by the message,

A special treat for someone special

IDEA # 77

Even if you are just going down the road to buy some milk, act as though you are returning home after a major adventure.

Say something like, "Well it was touch and go there for a while with the snow and the wolves but I made it!" and then give your partner a huge bear hug.

IDEA # 78

Send your partner a thank-you note. For example:

Dear Bec,

Thanks for helping me move house. Having you there made a huge difference. I really appreciate your help and your love. Tim

IDEA # 79

If you have kids, organize for them to stay at their grandparents for the weekend.

On Friday evening, announce that the weekend is yours and start planning how you are going to spend your special time together.

IDEA # 80

Give your partner a magic gift box. Every month, place a new small gift in the box for her to discover.

IDEA # 81

Research your partner's favorite hobby and identify a gift that is really useful for her. The more specialized the gift the more impact it will have. Talk to her friends and family and use the Net to find the information you need.

IDEA # 82

Go to a masquerade ball. Send an invitation to your partner telling her to meet you at a specific spot at the stroke of eight.

Wear a mask and when you meet her, don't say a word. Just take her hand and lead her on to the dance floor.

IDEA # 83

On Thursday, ask your partner to pack a bag for the weekend. Tell her she'll need casual clothes and walking shoes but don't tell her what you have got planned.

Pick her up after work on Friday and drive to a romantic bed and breakfast for a romantic weekend of relaxation.

IDEA # 84

When you are relaxing at home one night, take two large sheets of paper and some pencils or crayons. On each piece of paper, draw the outline of a large crystal ball sitting on a stand.

Tell your partner to look into her crystal ball and draw what she sees five years in the future. Do the same thing yourself and then come together to share and discuss your drawings.

IDEA # 85

Create a loving nickname for your partner. This could be the name she was called by her family when she was a little girl or something that is special just for the two of you.

IDEA # 86

If you are musically inclined, write a love song for your partner. Call it something like "Natasha's Song".

Produce a professional looking manuscript, print it out and get it framed. Record your song onto CD and take a photo of your partner and get a print shop to create a CD cover if you can't create one on your computer.

Place the framed manuscript and the CD in a box and give it to your partner as a special gift.

IDEA # 87

Pick your partner up for a date and blindfold her before driving to a special destination.

Try to make the destination something really unexpected like a table set up at the top of a cliff or a dinner on a boat or old-fashioned ship. It needs to be something that will have an impact when she removes the blindfold.

IDEA # 88

Have a really big pillow fight. Set up for it by buying two pillows that are filled with feathers. Put holes in the pillows so the feathers will start to fly and then attack your partner when you feel the time is right.

IDEA # 89

Get out into the great outdoors. After a day of hiking, build an open fire. Sit by the fire with your partner, toast marshmallows and watch as the embers of the fire climb into the night sky.

IDEA # 90

If your partner uses a computer, take a photo of the two of you and get it scanned at a print shop (or scan it at home) and store it on disk as a .bmp file.

Transfer the file onto your partner's computer and set the image as the computer's wallpaper.

To do this on a Windows machine, select Start / Settings / Control Panel / Display. Choose the Background tab and click the Browse button to find your .bmp file.

IDEA # 91

If you are artistically inclined, do a life drawing course, practice until you are confident and then ask your partner to pose for you.

IDEA # 92

Take your partner to a carnival or festival. Try the following:

1. Food festival
2. Jazz festival
3. Wine festival
4. Music festival

IDEA # 93

Develop a video time capsule. Start with the two of you sitting together on a couch introducing the video. Say something like, "It is currently July 14th 2002. We have decided to make this video so that we can watch it together on our 25th wedding anniversary."

Then have a section where you talk to the camera by yourself, telling the camera how you feel about your partner and why you love her. Get her to do the same thing. When you are done, place the video in a bank vault and on your 25th wedding anniversary you will be able to look back in time and reminisce about everything that you have shared.

IDEA # 94

If you are in a secluded spot near a beach or lake and the weather is warm, go for an impromptu skinny dip with your partner.

IDEA # 95

This one is great for long distance relationships. It takes a bit of organization but if you can pull it off, it is sure to be a surprise that your partner will never forget. Organize to catch up with her regularly over the internet using either a chat room or an Instant Messenger program. Then arrange a secret trip to meet her without telling her that you're coming.

When it comes time for your usual chat over the Net, arrange for a close friend back home to log on using your nickname while you position yourself outside her door. Phone your friend on your mobile and be speaking to him in real time. Tell him to type in the following sentence, "I really miss you honey, I wish I could be there and just reach out and knock on your door." As soon as he has sent the message, knock on the door!

IDEA # 96

Buy your partner a gold fish in a bowl and give it to her with a card saying,

"Of all the fish in the sea, you're the fish for me!"

IDEA # 97

Go for a drive either early in the morning or at dusk. Get a CD/tape that contains sounds of nature such as Sounds Of the Rainforest and play it as you hold your partner's hand and drive.

IDEA # 98

The day before your partner's birthday buy some helium balloons, streamers and flowers and hide them in a closet.

When your partner has fallen asleep, string the streamers around the room and bring out the balloons and flowers. Place them around the bed so that your partner wakes up to a real birthday surprise.

IDEA # 99

Spend a leisurely afternoon with your partner in a large book shop such as Borders where you can browse the shelves, share a coffee and sit down to peruse your purchases.

IDEA # 100

If you can afford it, hire a sports car for a weekend. Pick up your partner and give her a long white cashmere scarf to wear with her sunglasses. Go for a drive along the coast with the top down.

IDEA # 101

Serve your partner breakfast in bed. Try the following:

A poached egg in the shape of a heart - you can pick up a heart shaped poacher at most shops that sell kitchen wares.

French toast with cinnamon and maple syrup.

Cereal.

Fruit juice.

A fresh flower.

Printed by Libri Plureos GmbH in Hamburg,
Germany